Woman

Ava Pie

ISBN 978-93-5610-529-4
© Ava Pie 2022
Published in India 2022 by Pencil

A brand of
One Point Six Technologies Pvt. Ltd.
123, Building J2, Shram Seva Premises,
Wadala Truck Terminal, Wadala (E)
Mumbai 400037, Maharashtra, INDIA
E connect@thepencilapp.com
W www.thepencilapp.com

DISCLAIMER: *The opinions expressed in this book are those of the authors and do not purport to reflect the views of the Publisher.*

Author biography

Ava Mary Pie (she/they) is an adult high school student and independent musician. They are a mom to 13 fur babies, who make up her whole world.

CONTENTS

SLUT

I wear slut like a badge of honour
A title bestowed upon me for not meeting archaic patriarchal standards of purity and meekness
So, yes I am a slut if you'd like to call me that
If that makes you more comfortable when dealing with a women who's comfortable with and in charge of her own sexuality and body
I'll admit that I'm a goddamn whore and proud of it
I'm the slut who'll talk about her terrible anal sex experience at your dinner party and gross you all out with tmi, details and hand gestures, yet never flinch about that being her first time having penetrative sex
I'll feel no shame in recounting graphic details, that is, only if you're comfortable, of course
I'm the slut who posts lingerie and shower pictures on my social media, tastefully blurring out the bits that would get me reported
I'm the slut who'd be so triggered and withdrawn if her nudes leak and make sure the hacker gets their due but would never blame herself or let anybody blame her
And I'm the slut who would retailiate with making her best friend take even better nudes and post them herself even though all she wants is to never take off a single thing again
I'm the slut who has sex in cars and trial rooms and

terraces and cinema halls when the sex she's having is illegal in itself

I'm the slut who laughed out when her mom walking in on a steamy half naked make out session, even though the thought made her cringe and want to cover up

I'm the slut who looks her boyfriends Indian parents in the eye as they curiously inspect the dark hickeys all over his neck

I'm the slut who kisses her beau at a busy airport filled with cisnormative homophobes and the moral police in front of her Indian mom and who bashfully looks away because he's leaving and she wont let him go without a kiss goodbye

I'm the slut who brags about fingering her paramour to La La Land and then busting out of the screen to make out in the washroom

I'm the slut who wore no pants and just a shirt with wet underwear on a long cab ride home at night without a second thought because her leggings were soaked and she didn't have a spare

I'm the slut who lives in shorts and crop tops and never tucks in her bra or straps and always swims in string bikinis in crowded Indian pools

I'm the slut who walks around empty streets past midnight and takes cabs alone down empty streets, late, in a cleavage baring dress, still a little drunk from the party I just went to

I'm the slut who'll get wasted in a dive filled with creepy men eyeing me up and down and not let them ruin my night with their lack of respect for my personhood

I'm the slut who'll show the guy who hit on me when I was drunk and alone a middle finger from my auto as I'm leaving the place

I'm the slut who'll casually discuss my past sexual assault with you right after we've had some passionate sex
I'm the slut who's not afraid to smack your hands away from me if I feel uncomfortable
I'm the slut who will make sure you're enthusiastically consenting and comfortable and ask for permission every step of the way
I'm the poly slut who will kiss other men and women and all the other genders on the spectrum and tell her partner about it and make sure they're cool before she does
I'm the slut who will talk about orgasms and masturbation and sex on social media, in parties, with her mom, in her writing
I'm the slut who demands to climax, to be respected, to feel good every time she is touched
I'm the slut whose best work is erotic, about bodies, about sex and about sluttiness
I'm the slut who will wear anything like a dress if it's one inch lower than where her panties come to an end
I'm the slut whose partners and best friends lovingly call her a hoe and vice versa
I'm the slut with hoe in all of my social media bios
I'm the slut who's had her share of hook ups, friends and crushes, boys and girls and enbies alike
I'm a slut because cleavage baring is a way of life for me and I'm proud of the boobs I was once made to feel bad about having
I'm a slut because I feel sexual desire and I dare to express it, dare to seek and find satisfaction
I'm a slut because I talk about primal urges and natural things that everybody feels and does
I'm a slut because I overcame a slew of insecurities and

now I dare to love and celebrate my body in its stripped down natural form on social media

I'm a slut because I dare to challenge archaic double standards and patriarchal notions and desecrate them

I'm a slut because I have no fucks to give about your damaged moral code or idea of decency or so called culture

I'm a slut because that's what we do with outspoken opinionated women - we label them and shame then and try to crush their spirits

Yes I'm a slut but you could be too

If you drink, if you smoke, if your bra falls out a little, because of your clothes, because of your sex life, because of your rape or your abuse

Because of allegations, because you're outspoken, because you have too many children with your husband, because you have a lot of guy friends

Because you are a woman, cuz that's the one that really counts isn't it

The only common thread in all these different things that apparently make different people sluts

Anything could make you one, really

As long as you're a woman

You can spend your life making every effort to fit all these unmeetable standards they place upon us and be the meekest good girl stereotype

And they'll still find a way to label you a slut, by virtue of your birth, your body, your breasts,your penis, your vagina, your clitoris

We're all sluts and bitches in their eyes

Too big for our britches

Too sexual, too loud, too human, too honest, too real, too

sexy, too plain, too bold
Fuck their bullshit standards and their unfair dichotomies
Fuck their judgement and ignorance and shaming and hate
Fuck their opinions
You do you girl
Wear slut like a badge of honour
Wear bitch like a mark of pride
Wear cunt with even more honour for vaginas are not something to be ashamed of, and neither is standing up for yourself
Wear your sexuality and your body on your sleeve with your head held high and your middle fingers up
Wear your sexual history around your neck with no shame and make no apologies for demanding and talking about your pleasure
Be a slut, be a whore, be a self professed bitch
And never apologise for it
Touch yourself, touch others, be touched
But make sure everybody's consenting and comfortable
Demand respect, demand comfort, demand pleasure, demand dignity
Always be in charge, you have power, you have authority
Fuck yourself, fuck others, be fucked
And make sure to tell the haters to fuck off while you're at it
Baby girl you can't win in this patriarchal world
But the only way to fight it is to not play into what they want from you
Let them call you names, let them hate, let them point their fingers
You just continue to be and do you
While they point fingers use yours to get yourself off

While they splatter your name in red, use it to cover your naked body, only enough for your comfort but little enough to make them uncomfortable
Don't let anybody make you feel like you don't have a right to these things because you do
Even if it takes being called a lot of names while you get there
Build castles out of the bricks and the mud they fling your way
Build fortresses around you and keep them locked out permanently
And if this sexist world is getting you down and you need some company
Baby girl you can always come talk to me
We will vent we will rage we will never back down
Someday the sluts will be the ones wearing the crowns
And if you ever feel like being who you are makes you less amazing or worthy
I hope you remember you're not the only slut who's ever felt that way, and I hope you think of me
Read my poems, see my pictures
And know you're not alone
And if you ever need to talk about it
Just hit me up on my phone
I'll build you up and remind you that you're a ground breaking feminist rebel
That your mere existence is revolutionary and in this you must revel
You must seek no approval, never apologise or grovel
Nor giving fucks is a practised art that takes its time, but don't worry some day you'll be at my level

BITCH

I am a bitch, why thank you for pointing it out
I am a raging spitfire and who spews venom
Bitch rolls off your tongue almost as neatly as behenchod
rolls off mine
And that's really saying something
My go to words for friends and lovers would make your
grandma blush and your mom curse mine
I embroider my sentences with all the fucks I don't give,
for emphasis of course
I never hold my tongue when it comes to speaking my
mind
Rants and critiques with no short supply of biting phrases
and cuss words
This world can't handle a strong capable woman who
doesn't care what you think
She had to be torn down and labelled and degraded
This world can't handle a woman who dares to act like
men have been acting since the dawn of time
He's a boss and he's the man but she's bossy and has
forgotten her place
Maybe she's too much of a woman for you to handle
Too strong, too rough, too irreverent, too revolutionary
Maybe that's what she is
And maybe that's what I am
So go on, call me what you like

Slut will not bother me
Bitch will not make me toe the line
Whore will not make me want to fuck you
Cunt will not make me feel ashamed
I am a bitch
I'm the bitch who will point it out when you interrupt me
in meetings
I'm the bitch who will not hesitate to call you out when
you're being sexist or racist or queerphobic
I'm the bitch who will clock you if you try to get fresh
I'm the bitch who'll turn down your harassment with witty
quips and post it everywhere with your name intact
Yes I'm that bitch
The bitch who will not hold her tongue
The bitch who will never swallow her pride
The bitch who will never meet your unfair expectations
The bitch who'll turn those expectations on their head and
point out the hypocrisy in them
The bitch who refuses to say silent
The bitch who refuses to play along
The bitch who can't take a joke if the joke furthers the
oppression of the already disenfranchised
The bitch who isn't afraid to make it personal and drag
your past actions into it
The bitch who isn't afraid, of you, or of anybody
And that's what it boils down to, doesn't it
Bitches are women who aren't afraid to speak their minds
Who aren't afraid of the patriarchy
Who aren't scared of anybody
Who don't have fucks to give about your opinions of them
And I guess that scares you, doesn't it
A woman you don't quite know what to make of and what

to do with
A woman you can't control and subjugate and petrify
A woman who's forgotten her place in this patriarchal fuckdom
A woman who is too much your weak little minds to fathom or comprehend
So you label me, shame me, do your best to tear me down and put me in my place
But you can't
Because I'm just too much of a bitch for that
Too much of a bitch to let your silly little opinions get to me
Too much of a bitch to change just so you're more comfortable
Too much of a bitch to know my so called place in this patriarchal world
Too much of a bitch to care, that's for sure
I'm a bitch, I'm a cunt, I'm a whore, I'm a slut
And I'm a person worthy of respect and love
Only from fellow feminists in the struggle, of course
Cause for this bitch when it comes to love, once it rains, it pours

MENSTRUATION

Oh monthly visitor
They hate you because you are feminine
You are abject, you break through this restrictive polished society we created
Just like excrement and giving birth and in some ways, sex
They hate you because they do not understand what you really are
They think you are dirty and say they censor you because you are blood
When they pay big money to watch violence and bloodshed on screen every weekend
The truth is they hate you because they know you as female
And feminine is lesser, women are dirty and unholy
I don't agree with any of them, I know they're all wrong
I hate you because I lose sleep every month for a whole week before you come
And it triggers mood swings and dysphoric mania arrives to ruin the day
I hate you because pads and period panties give me rashes and discomfort and tampons terrify me
I hate you because PMDD is a real thing and no one takes it seriously and doctors dismiss it and feminists, the ones supposedly on your side say it's made up when you know what you feel that time of the month when you're losing sleep and losing friends

I hate you because the pain you give me is worse than the
pain from burns and surgeries and scars and I have to pop
a bunch of pills and cry to make it bearable
I hate you because for some reason I lose interest in food
when you're set to arrive and when you do
I do like that you're abnormally light and go away in two
days, sometimes three
I do like that I am not restricted or discriminated against
because my uterus threw a fit over being childless yet
another month
I do like that some pantyliners feel like heaven sometimes
for a day or so
I do like shattering period stereotypes and myths and
telling everybody I'm on mine just to see, and hopefully
change their reaction to this
I do like making young girls feel comfortable with and
proud of their bodies and their blood
I do like menstrual art, there is beauty in everything, and
our shameful secret can make art
I do like going to the temples and attending pujas on my
period with my mothers approval, she thinks it's archaic
not to too
I do like free bleeding for my rashes, it's barely visible, and
the bed stains at night but it's my bed
But I don't like menstruation
And I don't like my period
And I never will
And I will relate to PMS and I do dread Aunt Flo
And I won't wear tampons
But I'm a feminist as much as you
I will fight to the death for periods to be less taboo
I just won't love them too

WOMEN DON'T EXIST FOR YOU

Women don't exist for you to look at
Or gawk at or grope or assault or abuse
Women exist to be people
They don't owe you prettiness
And they sure as hell don't owe you sex
They don't have to be as thin as you'd like them to be
They don't have to be pretty according to your archaic
standards
They don't have to smile for you
They don't have to be shaved and waxed and hairless
They don't have to be feminine
They don't have to have a vagina
I am woman, hear me scream
Watch me make sexist weak little men weep
I am woman, hear me yell
Will I ever be equal, time will tell
Women don't exist to cook for you
And press your feet and stroke that inflated ego
They don't have to return your affections
Or turn their heads to look at you
Or respond to cat calls and wolf whistles
Or accept your promposal
Or bring you coffee while they're more qualified than your
whole existence
Or save you from your mediocre boring life and enrich it

Or be your adventure
Or fulfill your fantasies
Or even acknowledge your existence
Women do not exist for your pleasure
Or amusement
Or as a hole to shove your ugly penis in
Or as a punching bag for your frustrations
They are human beings with feelings and desires
A right to orgasm and a right to consent
A right to their bodies
A right to their sexuality
A right to public spaces
A right to advance in their careers
A right to just fucking exist
A right to just be
Women don't exist for you, men
For you to leer at and jeer at and beat up and rape
Women are people
Just let us be
Some freedom, equality and a right to personhood is all we
really need

BIG GIRLS CRY

Big girls cry
When they can feel the heartbreak pounding in their chest
When the scars of their past get pricked by the thorns of
their present
When they relive their traumas through their favorite
movies and the "jokes" cracked by their friends
When they watch the hearts of their purest friends fall
down and shatter into tiny little pieces
When their little fur babies pass away and they miss the
sound their little paws pattering across the floor
Big girls sob and yell
When depression has reduced them into curled up balls on
mattresses
When their fucked up families drag them into their messes
When the dreams they dreamed ever since they knew how
to dream seem like far off goals for another lifetime
When hormones rage high and ice cream seems like the
only source of comfort
When childhood best friends turn frenemies and then turn
strangers as if it was all for nothing
Big girls lie
To spare feelings, to save hurt
To charm their way into hearts
To flirt their way into beds
To dance their way into offices

To spare themselves consequences
Big girls cheat
At bingo, at cards, on diets
At chores, at responsibilities
In religion, at recovery
And yes, sometimes, even in love
Even in relationships, even with no guilt
Big girls fight
Their families who think they know what's best for them
Their partners who think the same, and rare to mess with
their autonomy
Their well meaning friends who sometimes don't mean
quite so well
Their children who think their lives belong to serve them
And of course the patriarchy and the scores of men and
systems designed to keep them down
Big girls fuck up
They ruin relationships, moods and days
They ruin their own lives sometimes
Or the peace of mind of the ones they love
But sometimes they ruin the best things
Like the image people have of them as saints and the
expectations placed upon them
Big girls rage
When they are degraded and body shamed
When they are labelled for daring to express their sexuality
When they are shamed for having opinions
When they are seen and treated as less than human
When they're abused and victimised
Big girls cry, they lie, they sob, they fuck up, they rage, they
cheat
After all they're people, like you and me

I'll admit I've done my share of little girl tantrums as my
big girl fuck ups
And I'm sure you've done the same
We've all diverse and varied
Collectively nobody's to blame
But big girls cry, I promise
And for being multifaceted humans we feel no shame

MY VAGINA MONOLOGUE

My vagina is not a lock
And your penis is not the key
My vagina is not like a sock
It's not like you've put a foot in me
Why does my vagina become the talk
While your penis goes scot free
My vagina is taking a walk
It's not open for you, no siree

My uterus is not a clock
Ticking away for some baby
My uterus has got its lock
I'm on birth control, you see
My uterus becomes the talk
At every family party
My uterus does not need a doc
You do not get to lecture me

My legs are not two magnets
That must always stay locked
You could call them to be stagnant
But you'd soon be blocked
If I turned out unmarried and pregnant
I tell you no one would be shocked
But a penis will only enter me

Woman

When my world is meant to be rocked

My vagina contains no honour
That any man could take from me
It's not worth a price in dollars
Without consent it simply can't be seen
My uterus contains no swimmers
No one propagating a gene
In this fucked up game there are no winners
So discard it, just let us be

ENTITLED

So many people have felt entitled to my body
Entitled to touch me, where they please, as they please
Entitled to tell me what to wear and what to change
Entitled to cover up the parts they think only they should
we
Some by virtue of being family, some by virtue of being
lovers
And some simply because I am a woman
Here's the thing, .
This is my body
You may look at it
You may even admire it
But you must respect it
You may not touch it unless I want you to
And you may not cover it up unless I want to
And you may not touch it for your own pleasure,
discounting mine
And you may not degrade it with your irrelevant opinions
And you may not act like my clothes or existence is
consent
And you may not act like my consent is irrelevant
You have no claim here
No matter who you are
Only I do
For it is my body

And it is mine
And you are just somebody with no stake or ground
So take your opinions, take your morality, and take your
over eager hands
And keep them away from me at all costs, at all times
For you may feel entitled to my body and my choices
But I will never allow you to infringe upon what's mine

MISOGYNY

Women are meant to be covered
Their bodies undiscovered
By men's lustful eyes
Well I won't cover myself and you can't make me
Please never mistake me
For a woman who complies
Women are meant to be polite
And give weary men respite
With their huge bosoms
Well I'm gonna get a reduction
And it won't affect my seductions
And I say whatever to mind comes
Women are meant to be meek
And act like they're weak
To stroke a man's ego
But I was made of strength
Made to lead, not to bend
I wasn't born to follow
Women are meant to be directed
Not to be respected
Unless they act a certain way
But I will never follow a man
I will always do what a can
I know the game, I just refuse to play
Women are supposed to shrink themselves

That what it all boils down to, forget yourselves
Just live for men
But I willl never let myself shrink
I will read, I will scream, I will think
For myself and for all women

WHAT I NEEDWHAT I DON'T

I can open my own pickle jars
I can pay my own way in bars
What I need is an equal partner
Not someone who makes my life harder
I can book my own taxis
I can swipe my card, max it
What I need is a shoulder
And when she needs it I will hold her
I can open my own door
And pick my stuff off of the floor
What I need is understanding
Not fear of being the last one standing
I can get the tab for two
I can defend myself too
And I will thank her for her patience
For I can do shit for myself
I don't need anybody's help
What I need is communication
What I need is to be loved
I promise that's enough

SAFETY

I will take my safety for granted
I will travel alone in taxis with no underwear and half of
my breasts on display
Because I am not a second class citizen
I do not seek to live in a world where only men get their
way
I will not keep my legs closed
I will spread them for whomsoever I please
Trusting that they will not betray me
Trusting that they will do as they're told
I will drink in the later hours of the night
In clubs and pubs and bars with flashing lights
And then I will book my own taxi and make my way home
Not scared about the fact that I'm sloshed and alone
Maybe I'm idealistic or maybe I'm simply naive
But I choose to reject the notion of a world they have
provided me with
I didn't drink
It didn't save me
I didn't initiate things
It didn't save me
I didn't even have breasts
But it didn't save me
So why should your notions of safety save me
No pepper spray, no knife and no gun for that matter

Will stop someone from violating me until the morning
after
So why should I not have my fun and take my safety for
granted
Why should I sit in front of my lover without my legs
parted
Why should I not get intoxicated when tbe sun goes down
When assault can happen to even the most careful girl in
town
So let me take my safety for granted, even thought really
I'm always on alert
The world will never be ready for change, so let me take
the blow and be the first

I will take my safety for granted
I will photograph my legs when parted
I will not do what's expected
Every man will not be suspected
No this isn't a not all men rant
This poem has a strictly feminist slant
I'm just saying I'm done being afraid
And I'm not done with things to say
I will take my liberties as they are
I might even change in the back of that car
Carefree, elated, unafraid
Skipping down the path my foremothers paved
Stupid? You may say it and I will point out it's ableist
But shouldn't every woman get to live her life like this
I will not take into consideration
That I am not a man
If I want it, if I see it, if I crave it
I will just say that I can

If your only problem with my safety is that I'm a woman
Then maybe the fool is you
With rape taking place at every avenue and time of day
What is a woman to avoid and what is she to do
For I was a mere child when they stole my autonomy from
me
I didn't even know what sexual assault was and what it
would mean
So I will take my safety for granted
And not let men ruin anymore of my life
When it comes to these ideas of fear you've supplanted
I think I would prefer to just roll the dice

MOLESTATION

In the crowded metro cabin
I await molestation
Like it's inevitable
Like its an expected outcome of being around so many
men
Maybe because it is
And it shouldn't be
But by merely stating what is and shouldn't be
You risk getting branded a feminazi
Like speaking up is comparable to genocide
In so many angry mens little minds
In an elevator with a strange man
I fear molestation
Like it's imminent
Like its the only outcome of such a situation
Like a strange man won't keep his hands off me
But I was not molested in a crowded metro
Or in a solitary elevator, but in my own home
The place I ironically still feel the safest
Until a man invades its space
Maybe its unfair to cast my suspicions on every student or
worker who comes to my place
But men have created this fear, this frozen deer look on
my face
Men have created this culture

Woman

Where I'm afraid to step out of my home
And scared to fall asleep inside of it
Men have taken from me my sense of safety
Something I'm entitled to as a human being
Sitting next to my lover of more than a year
I don't even think about molestation
And that's when it happens to me
I don't shed a single tear
Just wonder how I got into this situation
Of this body I long now to be free

UNDERESTIMATED THE WRONG BITCH

You mistook me for a fragile helpless baby
When im really just a little slow, a little soft and lazy
You mistook my femininity for passivity and my sensitivity for weakness
You didn't know that the rage fire in my soul is so much stronger than the fire between my legs
You misinterpreted my silence as acceptance and my fear as compliance
You reprogrammed me to your tastes, like a malfunctioning appliance
And you pushed me and pushed me to the point of no return
So now im standing at the top of the mountain watching all of our memories burn
Don't underestimate a girl with long hair and soft pink dresses
Because a cold heart and ugly rage may caress her locks and tresses
Don't be fooled by the smiles and the cheery fables
Right when you think you've won, she may just go and turn the tables
You judge me by the way i dress, you judge be my stature
So you watch in surprise as i burn you in front of

everyone's eyes and no vengeance served has ever been greater

MEN ON SOCIAL MEDIA

Men on social media court me
Try to appease me or at the very least,
Try to get in my pants
I wake up every morning to a 'dear I wanna fuck you'
Or a 'can I lick your pussy'; gosh, how polite!
Some ask me to get more naked
Some simply show their love with their striking appendage
You can call it harassment but I call it attention
What girl wouldn't wanna wake up to this
I know it's because I put myself out there
Sexy pictures, yes
But wait, the texts are everywhere
Since before I posted anything below my shoulder length
hair
Okay fuck the sarcasm, I'm done
If you didn't read between the lines, you're probably scum
too
These men undress me with their eyes
It kinda makes me wanna cover up sometimes
When my natural instinct has always been to show skin
But I'd rather not get harassed if that's alright
Attention isn't supposed to make your skin crawl
There's healthy flirting and then there's a motherfucking
bar brawl
It's not a compliment to watch bloody, sweaty men turn

you into a prize
She's not horny bro look at the fear in her eyes, she's
fucking terrified
Being a woman on social media?
Yes but also nah
It's being an oppressed class in a kyriarchal world
So when men on social media court me
With dick pics and intentions of adultery
I block them, but first I take a screenshot
And let every other woman on social media see
To know who to avoid and who to put on that ever
expanding block list
If these men came at me face to face their ugly faces would
surely meet my fist
Honestly, these fools ain't worth a dime, much less a dollar
But I'll roast and expose them as long as they continue to
drunkenly holler

TEASE

I am a tease
I say what you wanna hear
I show what you wanna see
But when it all goes downhill
I can switch off my feelings and leave
I'm a serial dater
I'll go on a date the week I dump you
I'll make out with somebody the the day the last time I kiss
you
I am afraid
I don't open up enough to get hurt
So I turn off my feelings like a tap
But someday I will meet someone I can't shut down
Like you were
But I am a tease
And I say what you like to hear
I show what you like to see
But ultimately I'm going to leave

I DON'T DRESS TO IMPRESS

I dress to please my inner fashionista and critic
I don't have any airs or pretense of dressing to try to fit in
My plunge dress and ample bosom display is not to make
you drool
So if you take it as an invitation to harass me you're way
off base and way uncool
I dress for sweet compliments from all my female friends
Not to keep up with some industry or buy into the trends
But most importantly, I don't dress for men
Never have, never will, I don't even consider them
I don't dress to impress men and drive them wild
But they've been objectifying me for my outfits since I was
a child
I don't want men to stare at me, leer at me or pass lewd
comments on my body
So if you try that shit, you're messing with the wrong bitch
and I promise you're gonna be sorry
I don't want a sign around my neck that says invitation for
sex
All I'm asking for is basic human decency and a little
respect
I don't dress to impress anybody so keep your non
constructive feedback to yourself
I can't control the world around me but I will do whatever
I can to grab these notions and dispel

FEMME FATALE

You're just a manifestation of my sexual frustration
I don't need you, I need an island vacation
But if you were to tag along, would that be so wrong
I haven't had a primal connection in so long
You're just a droplet of water in the ocean that I swim in
You think I'm the trophy but you're the prize I win
I'm never being sincere and I'm being honest here
I just need a warm body to be on top of, under, or near
You're just another pawn in a game that you don't understand
If you don't pick up on my clues faster you'll be forcing my hand
But i will leave you wanting more, with your body aching and sore
I am many things, not all of them good, but I'm never a bore
They call me femme fatale, they call it lethal femininity
I say it's all part of my charm and my burning sensuality
I will leave you in the lurch to lick your own wounds and hurt
After its all over you can expect me to be curt
They call me feminine destruction because of what I leave in my wake
And sometimes you'll think being seduced by me was a rookie mistake

But you can find me among the stars and in the passenger
seat of pretty cars
I'll find my next victim or conquest at the bar
I don't drink but I will imbibe your juices
I'm an enigma that attracts and confuses
I don't smoke but I'll inhale your vapours
And you'll never get me to sign marriage papers
Yes I am a femme fatale and yes you are my target
But my sweet loving that one night, you'll never forget
Yes I am the destroyer and you my sweetest destruction
So maybe you should think twice before you give in to my
seduction

INEQUALITY

In a world where most abusers are never put to justice
And survivors receive little empathy or solace
And the statistics are skewed, men on women
How can you take me and you, man and woman
And say that we are equal at last
This is just a sequel to the past
Equality is merely a pipe dream in a world where little girls
have to fight bullets to study
Where survivors of rape cannot access abortions and often
die of back alley caused sepsis
Women are expected to change their names and identities
to belong to a man and his family
I've yet to find a man who would do the same willingly and
happily
When things cost more for women and they have to bear a
pink tax
Which comes on too of everything else, which makes
shopping for daily needs a daunting task
There is a wage gap, less pay for the same jobs by the same
boss
And women of minority races suffer an even bigger salary
loss
Femininity is looked down upon for all genders while
masculinity is heralded
All these gender roles and outdated tropes have just made

me exhausted
Guys who have casual sex are cool dudes, studs, players and more
While girls who do the same are sluts, their bodies are no longer pure
Our bodies are objectified and receive endless judgement, leering, harassment and criticism
While men walk around shirtless and scratch their balls in public in boxers, you can't miss em
Even if both spouses work equally hard, the woman is expected to take care of the household and children
And when a man does his tiny part, it's ridiculous how much praise and adoration he is given
When a man is bad at something, he is bad at something
But when a woman is bad at anything, all women are bad at that thing
The inequality and sexism that still exists is depressing and disgusting
I, for one, pledge to spend my whole life trying to change a part of this

ITEM SONGS

Even when a woman is in complete control of her
sexuality, she is termed an item
She is expected to be tall and fair, with ample bosom to
spare, and of course - slim
She must still depend on a man for money, housing and
transport
Then be blamed and shamed when the marriage doesn't
end well and she needs to collect spousal support
Sheila was known for her flair, sure, but she was mostly
known for her youth
Without a crease in her saree, blemish on her face, or a
single yellow tooth
These songs fill a demand in a saturated market of lust
filled men
I believe that this will change someday, but I honestly
couldn't say when
Maybe when lines about harassing a youthful beauty will
go out of style and feel dated
In a culture that thrives on your objectification, it's hard
not to feel used and hated
My feet still tap to the beats and i dance on lyrics that
further my oppression
Because it's inescapable, at every party and wedding, on
every radio station
I can't help but sing along to words that I know are wrong

and sometimes I make them more empowering
And sometimes I slip my name inside the track as i groove
and sing while I am showering
But I am not an item, no matter what I wear or sing
I am a full human being and everything
I am not an object, and that's not for them to decide
Because I raise a finger to their laws and labels and simply
refuse to abide

TAYLOR SWIFT

Her name used to be synonymous with teenage
sentimentality
Today it is synonymous with the entire American music
industry
She never publically claimed her title, but she remains one
the queens
The rest of us must accept life through her benevolent
reigns
She is beauty, she is grace, with not one single hate
comment out of place
The contentment that she now feels inside shows up as a
quiet glow on her face
Her body is not cookie cutter perfect and this has at times
given her some distress
And she's not perfect either and has slut-shamed an ex
boyfriends new paramour or mistress
But she's been vocal about it and helped the rest of us feel
more normal
And her apologies for the moral policing showed that
apologies can be sincere and informal
Taylor Swift is her name, and she commands respect when
she walks into a room
She doesn't feel the need to settle down for children or
make her beau into her groom
Her kindness and sense of humour has won my Swiftie

heart
I will forever dissect, discuss, share, opine and pine over all
of her art
For she is the reason I felt empowered to pick up the pen
and write my own music
Although when I look back at the songs I wrote then,
they're rather silly and embarrassing
But now I write all my own songs and have hits to my
name, and she is the one to thank
She's the first one I'd DM the minute I got fame, because
for her, the space in my heart will always be blank

PINK

Never was there a colour invented so polarising as the colour pink
Boys don't dare to touch it, because after all, what would people think
It makes for delicious fruits, desserts, and even drinks
But if a man dares to enjoy any of those, he will be made fun of with subtle winks
It indicates weakness and femininity
Sometimes liking it is even mistaken for immaturity
Why must anything associated with femininity be associated with ridicule and weakness
When we know that femininity can also be tough, can also mean strength
A colour is a colour when it boils down to it, and it's not meant for a gender
When it comes to colours and ridiculous symbolism, pink is the highest contender
I have always loved strawberries and pink flavoured things, pink coloured items
And I have been made fun of for daring to sport them, and like them
But I do not care, I am not ashamed of being a feminine stereotype
Because I see strength in women, and I don't believe we can be condensed into a prototype

I like strawberry wine, and flamingo pink walls in my living
room
But if you wanna stereotype me based on that, I'd urge you
not to assume